Learning Sharks

Joseph Otterman

✹ Smithsonian

© 2019 Smithsonian Institution. The name "Smithsonian" and the Smithsonian logo are registered trademarks owned by the Smithsonian Institution.

Sharks are big fish.
They have big teeth.

3

Sharks are good swimmers. They are good smellers too.

5

Sharks need a lot of water. They swim and swim.

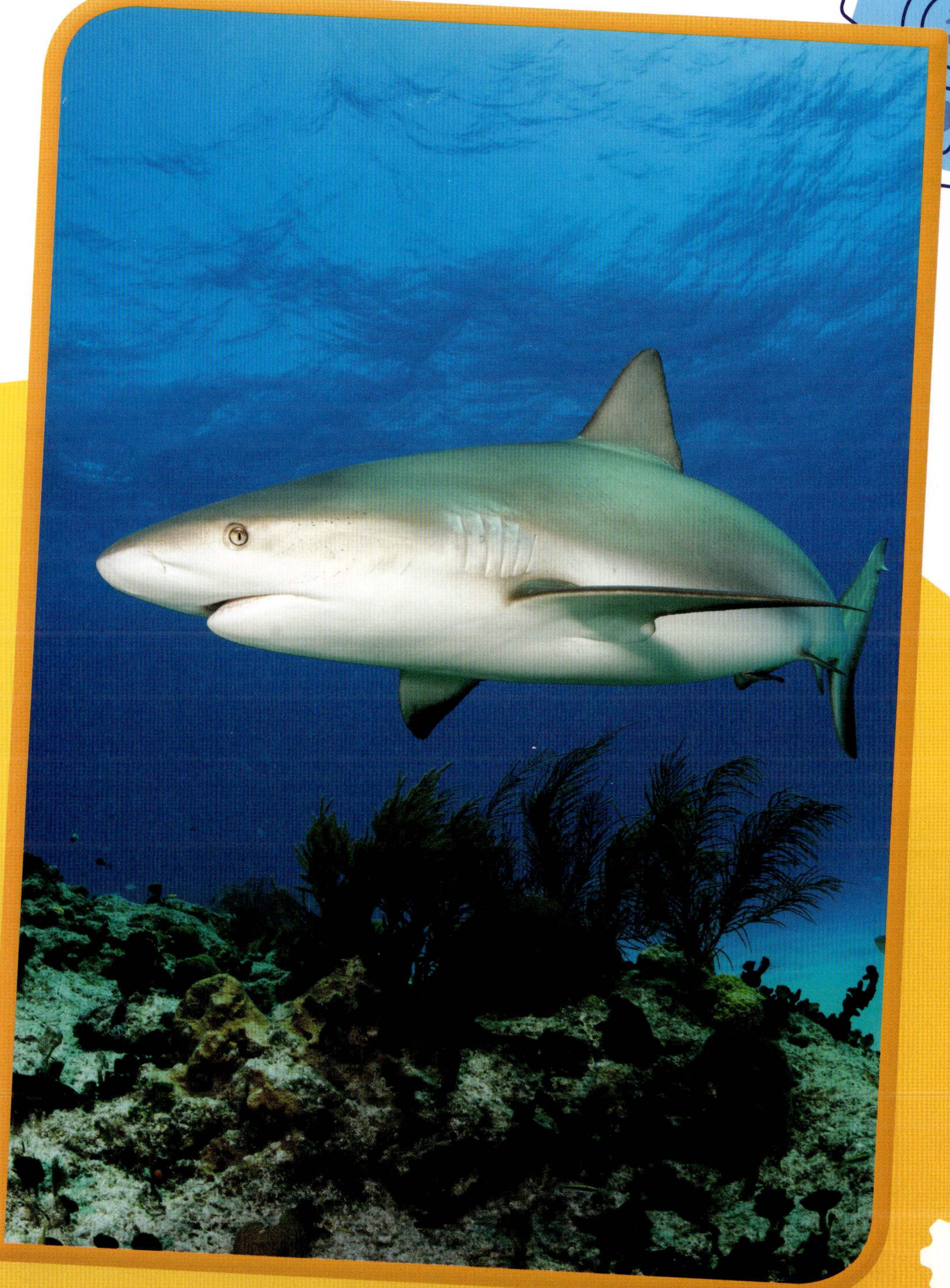

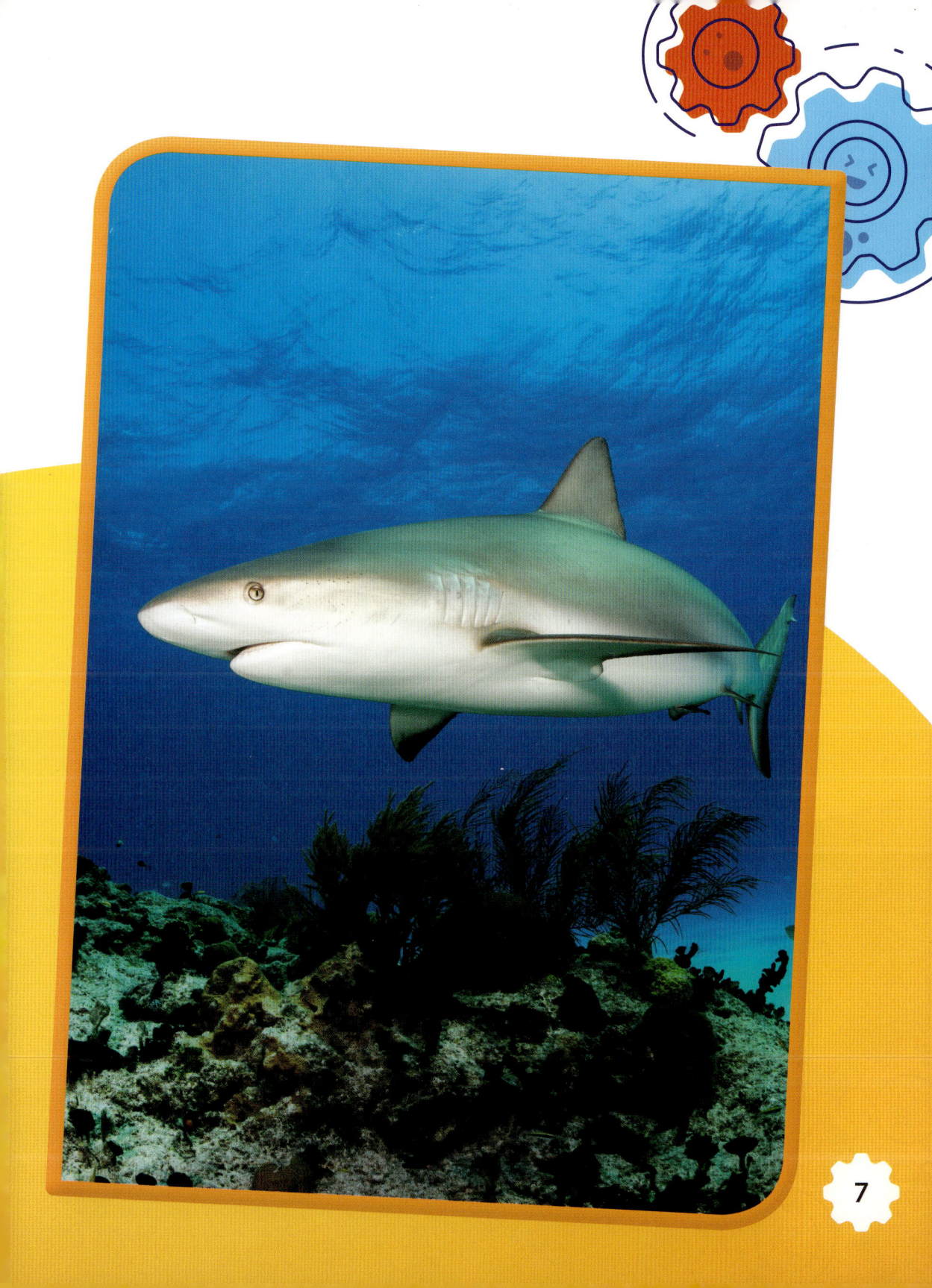

Sharks need a lot of space. They hunt and hunt.

9

Sharks need a lot of food. They eat and eat.

11

We can learn about sharks. We can watch them.

13

We can learn more about sharks. We can track them.

a tracker

We can film sharks in the water!

17

STEAM CHALLENGE

The Problem
You want to study an animal. How can you watch it without being seen?

The Goals
- Make a screen so you can observe an animal.
- The animal should not see you.

1 Research and Brainstorm

Learn about sharks.

2 Design and Build

Draw your plan. Build your screen!

3 Test and Improve

Use the screen to observe an animal. Then, try to make it better.

4 Reflect and Share

What did you learn?

Consultants

Amy Zoque
STEM Coordinator and Instructional Coach
Vineyard STEM School
Ontario Montclair District

Siobhan Simmons
Marblehead Elementary
Capistrano Unified School District

Publishing Credits

Rachelle Cracchiolo, M.S.Ed., *Publisher*
Conni Medina, M.A.Ed., *Editor in Chief*
Diana Kenney, M.A.Ed., NBCT, *Series Developer*
Emily R. Smith, M.A.Ed., *Content Director*
Véronique Bos, *Creative Director*
Robin Erickson, *Art Director*
Stephanie Bernard, *Associate Editor*
Mindy Duits, *Senior Graphic Designer*
Smithsonian Science Education Center

Image Credits: p.15 Pete Oxford/Minden Pictures/Getty Images; p.17 Jeff Rotman/Science Source; all other images from iStock and/or Shutterstock.

Library of Congress Cataloging-in-Publication Data

Names: Otterman, Joseph, 1964- author.
Title: Learning about sharks / Joseph Otterman.
Description: Huntington Beach, CA : Teacher Created Materials, Inc., [2020] | Audience: Age 5. | Audience: K to Grade 3.
Identifiers: LCCN 2018055259| ISBN 9781493866328 (paperback) | ISBN 9781425859770 (eBook)
Subjects: LCSH: Sharks--Juvenile literature.
Classification: LCC QL638.9 .O88 2020 | DDC 597.3--dc23 LC record available at https://lccn.loc.gov/2018055259

Smithsonian

© 2019 Smithsonian Institution. The name "Smithsonian" and the Smithsonian logo are registered trademarks owned by the Smithsonian Institution.

Teacher Created Materials

5301 Oceanus Drive
Huntington Beach, CA 92649-1030
www.tcmpub.com
ISBN 978-1-4938-6632-8
© 2019 Teacher Created Materials, Inc.
Printed in Malaysia
Thumbprints.21248